Bob Chilcott

Songbook

9 SONGS FOR MIXED VOICES

MUSIC DEPARTMENT

OXFORD
UNIVERSITY PRESS

OXFORD
UNIVERSITY PRESS

Great Clarendon Street, Oxford OX2 6DP, England
198 Madison Avenue, New York, NY, 10016, USA

Oxford University Press is a department of the University of Oxford.
It furthers the University's aim of excellence in research, scholarship,
and education by publishing worldwide

Oxford is a registered trade mark of Oxford University Press
in the UK and in certain other countries

Database right Oxford University Press (maker)

First published 2006

ISBN 978-0-19-335571-2

Music origination by Enigma Music Production Services, Amersham, Bucks.
Printed in Great Britain on acid-free paper by
Halstan & Co. Ltd., Amersham, Bucks.

Contents

Composer's note

This collection includes a mixture of both original pieces and arrangements. 'Aka-Tonbo' dates back to 1983, and was originally written for the vocal group The Light Blues for their tour of Japan. 'The Runner' is taken from a set entitled *The Modern Man I Sing*, composed in 1990, and was written for the choir of Gustavus Adolphus College, Minnesota. It was my very first paid commission for an original choral work! 'Composed upon Westminster Bridge', 'Dance in the Street', and 'Over the Wave' are also taken from larger works, and 'The Lily and The Rose' is a reworking of a piece that I originally wrote for children's choir. The three folksong arrangements, 'Ar Hyd y Nos', 'The Skye Boat Song', and 'O Danny boy' were written to be featured within the famous *Fantasia on British Sea Songs* by Henry Wood, and were first performed at the BBC Last Night of the Proms in 2005.

I am very grateful to Jane Griffiths for her work on this volume.

Aka-Tonbo

Rofuu Miki
(1889-1964)

KOSAKU YAMADA
(1886-1965)
arr. BOB CHILCOTT
(b. 1955)

*Keyboard reduction for rehearsal only.

English prose translation:
The red dragonflies fly at sunset. When I was young, and riding on nanny's back, I saw them. We picked mulberry fruits into a little basket in the field of a mountain. Or was it just a dream? At fifteen she married and was gone. Letters never seemed to come. The red dragonflies fly at sunset. Look, one now rests on a bamboo stick.

This piece is also available arranged for SAB *a cappella* in *Songstream 1: 10 Songs for Youth Choirs* (ISBN 978–0–19–343545–2).

Printed in Great Britain

OXFORD UNIVERSITY PRESS, MUSIC DEPARTMENT, GREAT CLARENDON STREET, OXFORD OX2 6DP

-ki,   o-sa-to-no ta-yo-ri-mo__ ta-e ha-te-ta.

(oo)

(oo)

-ki,   o-sa-to-no ta-yo-ri-mo__ ta-e ha-te-ta.

Yu-ya-ke ko-ya-ke-no

(oo)__ mm__   mm__

(oo)__ mm__

mm__

for the BBC Last Night of the Proms 2005
and dedicated to Serendipity and the BBC Symphony Chorus

Ar Hyd y Nos

John Ceiriog Hughes (1832–87)
English words: Sir Harold Boulton (1859–1935)

Welsh trad.
arr. BOB CHILCOTT

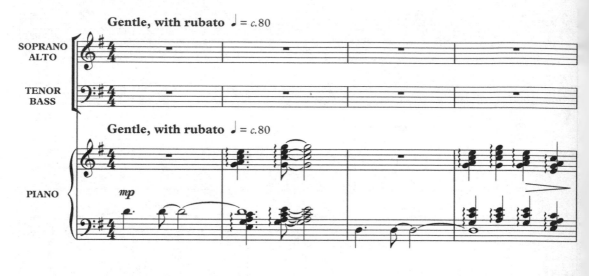

The orchestral accompaniment for this arrangement is available to hire from the publisher.

Composed upon Westminster Bridge,
September 3, 1802

William Wordsworth (1770–1850)

BOB CHILCOTT

This piece is also available in an arrangement for SATB and two pianos as the fourth movement of *Songs and Cries of London Town* (ISBN 978-0-19-343297-0).

Si - lent,   bare,   Ships,   to - wers,   domes,

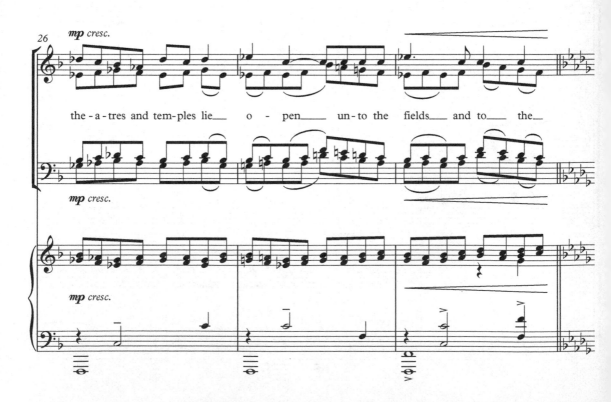

the - a - tres and tem - ples lie___ o - pen___ un - to the   fields___ and to___ the___

Ne'er saw I, never felt, a calm so deep!

The ri - ver gli-deth at his

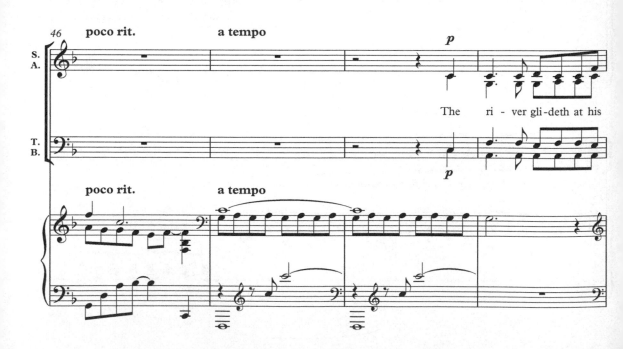

own sweet will;____ Dear__ God! the ve - ry____ hou - ses seem a -

- sleep;_____ and all that migh - ty heart is ly - ing

still!_____

for the Vasari Singers
in celebration of their 21st anniversary

Dance in the Street

Paul Verlaine (1844–96)
Free trans. by Bob Chilcott

BOB CHILCOTT

This is No. 1 of two pieces entitled *Dances in the Streets*. Both pieces, set to the original French by Paul Verlaine, are available separately (ISBN 978-0-19-343334-2).

for the BBC Last Night of the Proms 2005
and dedicated to Codetta and the BBC Symphony Chorus

O Danny boy

Fred Weatherly (1848–1929)

County Derry melody
arr. BOB CHILCOTT

The orchestral accompaniment for this arrangement is available to hire from the publisher.

An alternative arrangement of this piece for SATB and piano (entitled 'Londonderry Air') is available in
Encores for Choirs 1 (ISBN 978–0–19–343630–5).

gone, and all the ro - ses fall - ing, 'tis you, 'tis you must go and I must

bide. But come ye back when sum-mer's in the mea - dow, Or when the

val - ley's hushed and white with snow,_____ 'Tis I'll be there in sun-shine or in

sha - dow.   O   Dan - ny   boy,   O   Dan - ny   boy   I   love   you

so.

Dan - ny

And when you come   and all the flowers are   dy - ing,   If I am

26

boy,_____ O Dan-ny boy, Dan-ny boy.

dead, as dead I well may be, You'll come and find the place where I am

29

mp dolce

Dan - ny boy,_____ O Dan-ny boy. And I shall

div.

ly - ing, And kneel and say an A - ve there for me.

mp dolce

32

cresc.

hear tho' soft you tread a - bove__ me, And all my grave will warm-er, sweet-er

cresc.

mp cresc.

be,_____ For you will bend   and tell me that you   love__ me,   And I shall

sleep in peace un - til you come to   me,   you come to

me._____

Over the Wave

Native American (Ojibwa)

BOB CHILCOTT

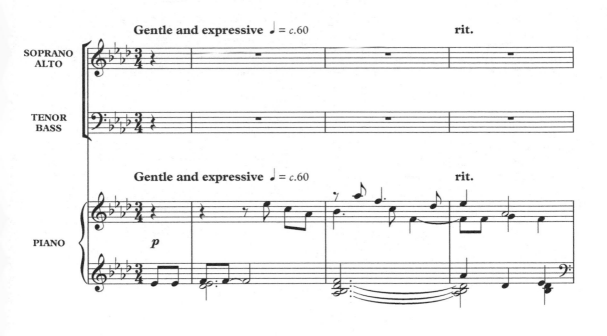

This piece is from *Circlesong: a life cycle based on Native American writings*, scored for SAB choir, SATB choir, two pianos, and percussion. The full work is available to hire from the publisher.

rip - ples glow.   But   I've   a   charm   that   can   make thee, dear,   Steal

o - ver the wave   to thy lo - ver here.

Who,   maid-en, makes this   ri - ver flow?   The

Spi - rit,   he makes its   rip - ples glow.   Yet   e - very blush   that   my

poco rit.   **a little slower**

make thee, dear,   Steal o - ver the wave _____ to thy

make thee, dear,   o - ver the wave _____ to thy

make thee, dear,   o - ver the wave _____ to thy

make thee, dear,   o - ver the wave to thy

poco rit.   **a little slower**

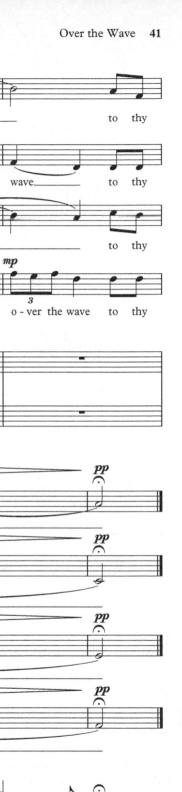

rit.   *pp*

lo - ver here. _____

lo - ver here. _____

lo - ver here. _____

lo - ver here. _____

mp   *pp*

This SATB version for Peter Hunt and the Berkshire Youth Choir

The Lily and the Rose

Anon. 16th-cent. English

BOB CHILCOTT

The original version of this piece, scored for upper voices and piano, is also available (ISBN 978–0–19–343317–5).

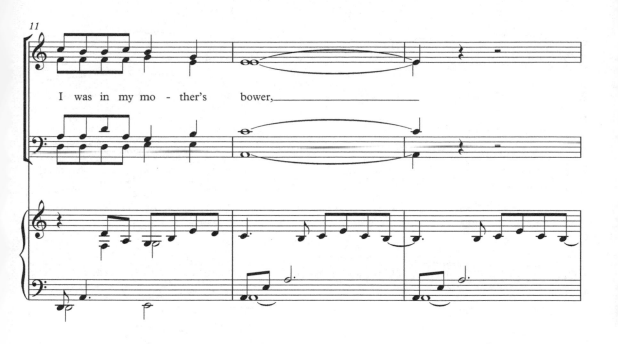

I was in my mo - ther's bower,_____

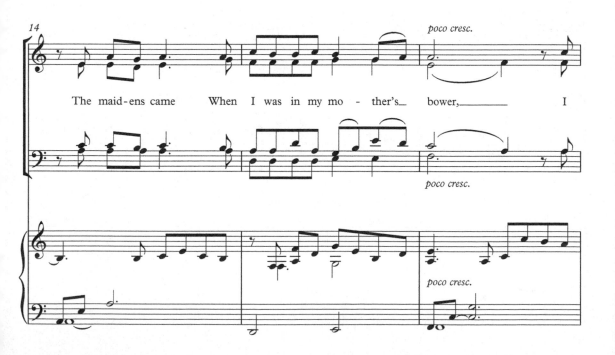

The maid-ens came   When I was in my mo - ther's__ bower,_____   I

poco cresc.

poco cresc.

poco cresc.

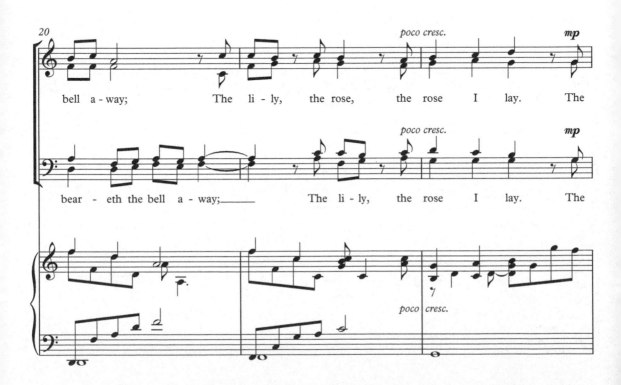

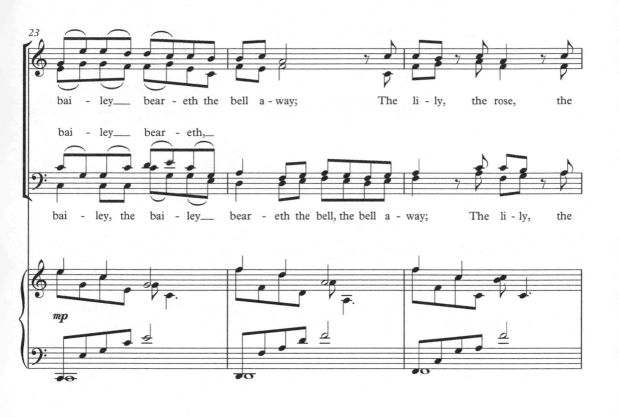

bai - ley___ bear - eth the bell a - way;   The li - ly,   the rose,   the

bai - ley___ bear - eth,___

bai - ley, the bai - ley___ bear - eth the bell, the bell a - way;   The li - ly,   the

mp

rose___ I___ lay.

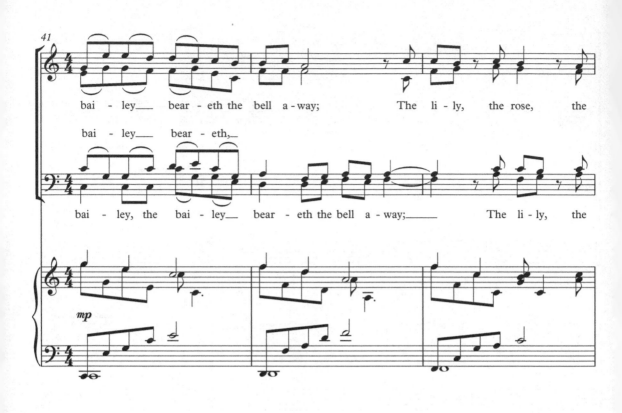

li - ly,   the rose,   the rose_____ I____ lay._____   And

- way;   The li - ly,   the rose_____ I   lay._____

- way;   The li -ly,   the rose_____ I   lay._____

poco più mosso

through   the glass_____   win - dows shines   the____   sun._____

poco più mosso

for Karle Erickson and the Gustavus Choir

The Runner

Walt Whitman (1819–92)

BOB CHILCOTT

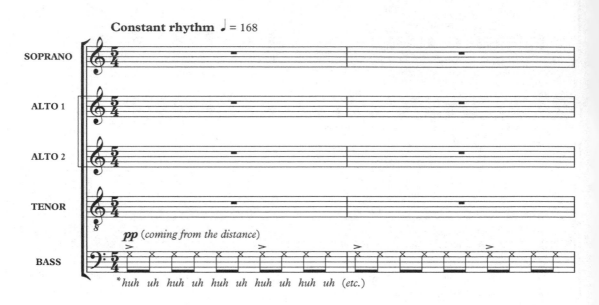

*Breathe in and out through mouth or nose, starting with an out breath, never too forcefully. Stop and start ad lib.

*Keyboard reduction for rehearsal only.

na   na   na   na (etc.)

huh uh huh uh (etc.)

a niente

for the BBC Last Night of the Proms 2005
and dedicated to the BBC Singers and the National Youth Choir of Scotland

The Skye Boat Song

Sir Harold Boulton
(1859–1935)

Scottish trad.
arr. BOB CHILCOTT

The orchestral accompaniment for this arrangement is available to hire from the publisher.

rend the air,_____ Baf - fled our foes

stand on the shore,_____ fol - low they will not dare._____

they will not_ dare.

Speed bon - nie boat, like a bird on the wing,

On - ward the sail - ors cry!

Car - ry the lad that is born to be king,

O - ver the sea to Skye!

Car - ry the lad   that is   born   to be   king,   O - ver the

sea_____ to   Skye!_____